Introduction

The railways around the South Coast emerged in early Victorian times and grew into a network of lines that still serve the areas of Hampshire and Dorset, which are the focus of this book. The emphasis is from the 1980s to present and illustrates what polished the rails during that time, with the journey commencing at Portsmouth Harbour station and ending at Weymouth, showing a broad spread of the varied trains that worked the lines there. My speciality is the Portsmouth area, since I live in Gosport and worked in Portsmouth Dockyard. John heralds from Beaulieu and has amassed a formidable collection of railway views from Southampton westwards to Weymouth, and indeed nationwide. John has also produced several series of railway books, and so he is the hand on the tiller as I navigate my way through what is my first attempt at showcasing my photographic collection.

My interest in trains started at a young age with a wind-up Hornby on the floor – sometimes without track! I can't remember how we happened on trainspotting at the age of eleven, but it was a real adventure getting on the bus to Fareham station. We thought it was amazing to see tracks seemingly going in all directions. I still remember standing there, awestruck, looking at the slab side of a Bullied Pacific with names of exotic places such as Watersmeet or Holsworthy with that lovely wavy West Country Class scroll. Oh no, I was hooked! So began an interest in railways that was to last to the present day.

Low points were to be getting a new ABC to find gaps where withdrawals had cut into loco classes and the headline that steam on the Isle of Wight was to finish soon. Luckily we had seen all the locos there some years previously, so to spare my disappointment I didn't cross the Solent for a last look. Also, by now, the fairer sex and motorcycling seemed more of an attraction. I suppose I was like lots of other steam fans – the end of steam was like a door closing.

A Portsmouth Dockyard apprenticeship passed and, after a few years, marriage and promotion too. Now working in an office for the Finance Department, I hit upon the idea of going to Victoria Park in my lunchtime. So there I was, sitting on a park bench facing the embankment that carries the line from Portsmouth Town High Level to the Harbour station.

Thus, the scene is set for what I didn't then realise was the revival of my interest in the contemporary railway scene. The 12.10 to Cardiff would rumble past and on one day it was headed by No. 33025, resplendent with the name *Sultan* on its bodyside. I thought to myself, 'Hmmm, they are putting names on locos again.' A visit to Commercial Road branch of W. H. Smith followed, a copy of Ian Allan's ubiquitous *ABC of Locomotives*; then, a line under *Sultan*'s entry. Lunchtimes would never be the same again!

I don't recall quite when it progressed to photography, but when it did, boy did it hit hard. I invested in a Zenith SLR and added a 135-mm lens, which, when I mastered the art of exposure reading, started get me better results. Most of the shots in this collection were taken with this camera. A Pentax ME Super was next, with the marvel of through-the-lens metering. Also, it was so much lighter! I roamed the tracks from the harbour and sought out every vantage point I could find using an old pedal bike, spending more time than I should have capturing as much of the passing scene as possible. Matching digital images to the photographs to identify the workings is a rather complicated process. Sadly, there was not always room for the date, which is annoying now.

What is amazing now is the variety of locos and stock that was paraded past the viewfinder in those heady '80s days. O8 shunters and Class 31s, 33s, 37s, 47s, 50s, 56s and 73s were abundant. Then, one day I spotted a Class 25 on the 12.10 to Cardiff. I walked out the main gate that day, thinking wouldn't it be nice to see something different and, lo and behold, No. 25069 came spluttering past. Argh! No camera with me that day!

I missed the Peak that came down one Friday too – a 138-ton test for the harbour girders!

Looking back now at the Sprinters that work to Cardiff, oh how I miss the Cromptons that started it all. Fratton Yard has been built on – well, most of it – and no more coal is taken there anymore.

I started using my Honda motorcycle to go to work. With my camera kept in the top box, this meant I could roam the trackside even further. Southampton and Eastleigh offered more delights, and it was on the Honda that I chased the last push-pulls to Weymouth.

Then, the unthinkable – a Bubble Car route learner started to appear most days and this heralded the new Class 155 Sprinters and the end of the 33's domination of trains to Cardiff. It's all progress, they say. Warships and Class 31s came and went, and freight action declined as well, so soon there was not much left to lure me to the lineside.

I must thank John Dedman for trawling through a mountain of negatives and scanning them into digital format, as well as for adding images from his considerable collection to the content of the book. None of this would be possible without his assistance.

The memories are still alive and the photographs bring it all back. I hope you enjoy the nostalgic journey provided by myself and John when we were both 'Wessex Rovers'!

Pete Nurse

RAIL ROVER
WESSEX RANGER

John Dedman and Pete Nurse

AMBERLEY

Front Cover top: EWS-liveried No. 66137 is seen at Marchwood on 4 August 2016 with 6B41, the 06.56 Eastleigh to Fawley. The tanks are carrying crude oil from the Holybourne oil field, near Alton in Hampshire. This service ended when the last train ran in September 2016, and unfortunately no loaded petroleum trains have run to or from Fawley refinery since. (JD)

Front Cover bottom: No. 33043 runs through Fratton station on its way to journey's end at Portsmouth Harbour station with a train from Cardiff. Two unidentified classmates, one of which will take the return service in an hour's time, stand on the fuelling road.

Rear Cover from top to bottom:
We are at the Fratton footbridge and the item of interest is No. 50018 *Resolution* as it rolls non-stop through the platforms, its train again slightly spoiled by the odd blue-grey second coach. The double arrow station sign certainly stands out above the train. (PN)

No. 47277, in Railfreight petroleum livery with smaller than normal cabside numbers, is seen at Pumpfield Farm level crossing at Marchwood with the 6B72 trip working from Fawley Refinery to Eastleigh Yard, which consists of four 100-ton BP TEA bogie tanks. 11 April 1990. (JD)

Looking over Racecourse Lane Bridge in a view made impossible now due the bridge having been extended to prevent vandalism, No. 47634 *Henry Ford* heads towards Cosham with the 10.08 Bristol Temple Meads to Portsmouth Harbour. Unusually, the train is made up of only three Mk 1 coaches.

No. 47316 has just passed under Horseshoe Bridge at St Denys with 6V79, the 09.07 Eastleigh to Severn Tunnel Speedlink. Included in the formation are MOD, cement, china clay and steel wagons. 19 September 1986. (JD)

First published 2019

Amberley Publishing
The Hill, Stroud
Gloucestershire, GL5 4EP

www.amberley-books.com

Copyright © John Dedman and Pete Nurse, 2019

The right of John Dedman and Pete Nurse to be identified as the Authors of this work has been asserted in accordance with the Copyrights, Designs and Patents Act 1988.

ISBN 978 1 4456 8065 1 (print)
ISBN 978 1 4456 8066 8 (ebook)

British Library Cataloguing in Publication Data.
A catalogue record for this book is available from the British Library.

Origination by Amberley Publishing.
Printed in the UK.

I first met Pete when he joined our local model railway club. He showed me some of his photographs, which included many from the Portsmouth area. My immediate thought was that it was a great collection, from what seems to be a little-photographed area in that time period. I have since used a few of his photographs in some previous books, but thought more should be published. So, with that in mind, we have included a good selection of Pete's photographs from the Portsmouth area before moving westwards on our journey. When compiling this collection, we have tried to include as many loco classes, liveries and types of trains as possible, as well as various locations.

We have also included a few images of traditional steam workings from the early 1960s, which included Eastleigh, Southampton Docks, the New Forest and the old route to Bournemouth via Ringwood. For these, I would like to thank Colin Rawlings for his monochrome images from the 1960s.

I travelled these routes in the school holidays in the early 1960s with the local Runabout ticket. One of my highlights was catching a train at Eastleigh in 1961, which went to Bournemouth West on the Old Road via Ringwood and Wimborne. This was the Sunday 12.40 from Eastleigh, and was hauled by a standard 4 2-6-0 in the 76xxx number series. At Bournemouth West we paid the Pullman supplement and rode to Southampton Central in style on the Bournemouth Belle.

For the lines beyond Bournemouth, we have very kindly been given some images by Mark Jamieson and Ray Kingswell, and would like to thank them for their contributions in helping to cover the Dorset area.

John Dedman

The journey begins! Portsmouth Naval Base is the background for this view, with Gosport beyond. The masts of HMS *Victory* are to the right. Here we see No. 33063 pulling swiftly away, a nice plume of exhaust giving ferry passengers a smoky walk up the ramp from the boat alongside the pontoon. The train is 1V62, the 12.10 Portsmouth Harbour to Cardiff Central. (PN)

Buffered up to the stock of the Plymouth to Brighton train is one of the really useful Class 73s. In the background, the masts of HMS *Warrior* can be seen, which had arrived at its permanent home after restoration at Hartlepool. The ED looks tidy in its InterCity livery, and the red coupling is a nice touch. (PN)

We are still at the Harbour station, with No. 33007 rumbling away as it waits for the clock to get to 12.10 so it can set off for the delights of Bristol and Cardiff. 4CIG unit No. 7367 on service 62 to Brighton waits to follow. (PN)

There is no mistaking the arrival of No. 50038 *Formidable* as it rumbles in with the Plymouth to Brighton train, its 117-ton bulk putting the girders to the test. Go back a few years and the thought of these marvellous machines being at the Harbour station would have been unthinkable. (PN)

One of Fratton Depot's 4CIGs rests at the buffer stops, but the real interest here is in the shape of No. 50027 *Lion*, which has just arrived from Plymouth. It is waiting for a Class 73 ED to take the stock the rest of the way to Brighton. We can still enjoy the delights and sounds of No. 50027 as it currently resides on the Watercress Line, still in Hampshire of course. (PN)

The service from Reading, in the hands of Hampshire Class 205 3H unit No. 1128, rolls along the embankment into Platform 1 at the Harbour. The London plane trees show off their new leaves and provide a nice backdrop to the scene. The remains of the spur to the Gunwharf are on the extreme right. Long since disused as a wharf, the area is now called Gunwharf Quays and contains a retail outlet. The 'Thumpers' plied their trade for many years to Salisbury and Reading, and their distinctive exhaust left you with no doubt as to what was coming. (PN)

Approaching the Harbour with the Plymouth to Portsmouth portion of the Plymouth to Brighton train we see No. 50045 *Achilles*. Looking very nice in its large logo livery, its grey roof is discoloured by soot from its four exhaust ports. The houses to the left of the loco would be best occupied by people with a liking for railways, I would think. (PN)

We move along the track a mile or so to Portsmouth & Southsea low level. Standing in the remaining platforms on a sunny evening, a Do It All DIY store now built over the others, No. 47634 *Henry Ford* is waiting with the evening mail. (PN)

An anonymous Rail blue Class 47 on blue-grey stock rolls down the steep ramp to gain level ground on the 11.55 Sunday Portsmouth Harbour to Liverpool train. The Do it All store has encroached onto the former rail land and spare stock is stabled to the left. Viewed through a 3-inch square hole cut into the footbridge, one risked looking like a drunkard kneeling on the floor to get a shot here. It was necessary, however, as the bridge's solid sides were too high to see over. (PN)

A little closer to Fratton, the aforementioned footbridge is in view, as is the Portsmouth power box. Unusually, a Crompton – which I believe to be No. 33065 – heads the Plymouth to Brighton train along the canal cutting towards Fratton in place of the usual Class 73. The 33 is unable to take advantage of the third rail's electric power, obviously. (PN)

It was a gorgeous sunny day on 2 July 1988 for the Portsmouth open day. Here we see the star of the show, No. 73130, which will be named *City of Portsmouth* after it reverses into the platform. Also in view are No. 37250 and Deltic No. 9000 *Royal Scots Grey*. Outside the station on a low loader was Terrier No. W8 *Freshwater*, from the Isle of Wight Steam Railway. Preserved 2BIL unit No. 2090 was also in attendance later. (PN)

The Wightlink ferries used to be supplied with fuel from tanks that were berthed in a siding on the side of the Harbour station. They were top and tailed from Fratton Yard to the harbour, and here we see No. 73141 taking the loaded tanks down with the 7P51 train from Fratton. The Class 47 on the rear will release the Class 73 before then taking the empty tanks away. This was the only freight working to pass this way with the demise of the dockyard's once-extensive rail system. (PN)

Passing the Portsmouth power box, a work-worn Crompton Class 33 rolls an incoming train from Cardiff along the canal cutting. Note the miniature snowploughs fitted to the loco. Back along the cutting, Somers Road crosses the line, and the bridge is another good spot for a photograph. (PN)

A good spot indeed! Here we can see a nice view of No. 47444 *University of Nottingham* as it passes under the Somers Road Bridge. The eight-coach train, with a BG at the front, comprises a blue-grey rake with one InterCity-liveried coach to break up the uniformity. The loco's large logo livery sits well and is my favourite. In this case, there was no chance of not being able to identify this locomotive. (PN)

Talking of InterCity livery, this image shows No. 47586 *Northamptonshire* in InterCity Swallow livery as it is about to pass under our old friend, the Somers Road Bridge, with a Portsmouth Harbour to Birmingham New Street train. This time, it has just one blue-grey coach. I had a day off and took this train to its destination for a day of photography, which was somewhat spoiled by the dark and gloomy New Street platforms. (PN)

One of the useful Class 73 electro-diesels accelerates its eight-coach train of Network SouthEast-liveried stock through the canal cutting towards the delights of Fratton. The majority of non-railway fans would probably disagree with this of course, failing to appreciate the charms of Fratton's station and yard. Note the ladder junction in the foreground. The loco headcode, 60, indicates a train to Brighton. (PN)

Looking nice in GWR anniversary green, No. 50007 *Sir Edward Elgar* is running an hour late due to a defective coach having to be removed at the harbour. The train is for Plymouth and the date is 7 October 1989. The loco still survives as *Hercules* and is back in blue again. This is a bit of a shame, but at least it is still in one piece! (PN)

I must have spent a lot of time near Somers Road Bridge, but there was a handy car park there within easy reach in dockyard lunchtimes. Let us feast our eyes on an attractive view of No. 33008 *Eastleigh* on IV62, the 12.10 Portsmouth Harbour to Cardiff Central, as it begins its journey. It was always nice to see the loco in its green livery. (PN)

Trains to Reading were usually in the hands of 3H DEMU Thumpers, but this is a Sunday and things have improved with the provision of 4TC No. 403, with traction provided by a Class 33/1 at the rear. Again, I failed to note the number and date, much to my chagrin. (PN)

What's better on a sunny day than to enjoy the view of a nice Class 50 in original Network livery hauling a train of matching coaches? Here, the view is slightly spoiled by the inclusion of a blue-grey coach in the line-up. The canal cutting reverberates with four exhausts as the loco works the 12.03 Pompey to Paignton. (PN)

Units in the erstwhile 'Jaffa Cake' livery were infrequent visitors to Portsmouth, but here 4CIG unit No. 1708 presents itself as it passes beneath Fratton Bridge, before proceeding to the harbour with a headcode 61 service from Littlehampton. (PN)

At the same spot as the previous view, and nicely backlit to show its InterCity livery (this variety being called Intercity Executive), No. 47839 looks marvellous with matching stock as it negotiates the curve from Fratton station and enters the canal cutting with the Wolverhampton to Portsmouth Harbour on 21 September 1987. (PN)

Moving on to the footbridge that crosses the platforms at Fratton, No. 47401 and the 12.30 Portsmouth Harbour to Birmingham New Street brings the doyen of the Brush Class 47s into view. Note the original number, 1500, on the front of the cab. Incidentally, this is one of my favourite photographs. 1 July 1989. (PN)

A nice change on the 12.10 Cardiff train as it runs into Fratton station is No. 31405, harking back to when they were regular visitors before the Class 33s took over. Emphasising their rarity are the haulage fans packing the front coach, including my friend Barry Andrews and his mate Dave. Baz is sadly missed, having collapsed and died on Cosham station many years later. (PN)

In an even better change, the 12.10 to Cardiff produced No. 37430 *Cwmbran* on 15 August 1987. This brought out the haulage fans yet again, who revelled in the tractor sounds these locomotives produced. (PN)

Entering Fratton station with the empty stock of an incoming train that has run on down to the Harbour station, Fratton shunter No. 08929 slowly draws into the loop to allow the loco to run round. The loco in question is framed under Fratton Bridge in the background. (PN)

Hampshire unit No. 1132 thumps its way towards Town station, or Portsmouth & Southsea if you prefer. Following on behind, with exhaust fumes filling the sky, No. 47615 *Caerphilly Castle/Castell Caerffili* is on an inter-regional service. (PN)

Observed passing non-stop through Fratton, electric unit No. 020 presents an intriguing image as it leads a four-car unit on service 60 (Littlehampton to Portsmouth Harbour). Unit No. 020 is a Class 931 two-car stores unit, comprising one coach from 2HAP unit No. 6044 and one from 4EPB unit No. 5302. (PN)

At Fratton Steam Depot, West Country Class No. 34026 *Yes Tor* is stabled in the yard in company with what looks like a S15 with a six-wheel tender. Looking at this now, I can't believe we didn't visit this wonderful place. We thought it was all electric units, so never bothered. Retrospect is a wonderful thing! (Colin Rawlings)

Oh what delights were contained within the roundhouse! Stored with possible preservation in mind are No. 30850 *Lord Nelson*, T9 No. 30120, No. 30777 *Sir Lamiel*, M7 No. 30245, Maunsell Q No. 30538 and Schools No. 30926 *Repton*. What a treasure trove! (Colin Rawlings)

Unusual locos turned up some lunchtimes and this one certainly quickened the pulse rate. Far from its Inverness home, and resplendent in ScotRail livery, No. 47541 *The Queen Mother* graces Fratton Stabling Point. The lamps are not fixed to the roof of the loco, but are just a regrettable clash. (PN)

A busy Fratton Yard with two Class 33s and a Class 73. Freights often changed locomotives here, with electro-diesel Class 73-hauled trains working east to Chichester, Hove and Three Bridges, before swapping with Class 33s and then working towards Eastleigh. Interestingly, the engineers' train looks to contain sand or sea ballast. (PN)

No wonder my pedal bike took me to this bridge! No. 33107 waits to leave with freight after having collected the two UKF pallet vans from its sister loco. The driver and shunter seem to be discussing the situation. (PN)

Slowly moving up the yard with another lunchtime freight are Nos 33022 and 33008 *Eastleigh*. They will proceed under my favourite footbridge to the ground signal and wait to be given the road to run up to Port Creek Junction. (PN)

The corrugated walls of the building make a different background to No. 47314 and its train of OTAs loaded with logs, which I believe were loaded in Chichester Yard. The loco is one of Tinsley's (Sheffield) allocation, as proclaimed by the Tinsley rose above the number. (PN)

We move on now to another favourite spot, where a view of No. 207010 is captured as it crosses Port Creek. It is about to take the left-hand line towards Cosham with a Reading train. The only problem here is that my back is to the A27, where it joins the M27, meaning it was impossible to hear the trains approaching because of the traffic noise. It was a pretty spot though. (PN)

I had seen this train running round in Fratton Yard; a mad dash up to Port Creek Junction and I was rewarded with a well-lit shot of No. 73005 *Mid Hants Watercress Line* in the late morning sunshine as it rattled over Port Creek, taking the Fareham line. (PN)

On the lunchtime freight from Fratton to Hove No. 73120 rumbles over Port Creek and takes the Havant line at the junction with a train of four TTAs, eight HEAs and three UKF pallet vans. This is 6Y53, the 11.39 from Eastleigh Yard, which will also call at Chichester Portfield Sidings. Just behind the junction sign my trusty Reliant Supervan II can be seen, which took me to lots of lineside locations. Luxury transport or what? (PN)

No. 73138 has a useful load of fourteen HEAs loaded with coal on the Fratton Yard trip to Hove. The driver is probably grateful for the extra power afforded by the juice from the third rail to the loco's traction motors. (PN)

Heading away from the junction at Port Creek on the line to Havant we see ED No. 73135 on fuel tanks and with just one HEA loaded with coal. I'm not sure if the tanks were bound for the fuel depot at Drayton the other side of Chichester. The busy A27 is in the left background. (PN)

A slightly work-worn but nevertheless attractive No. 33008 *Eastleigh* works 6Y51, the returning 10.00 Hove to Eastleigh Yard, which has called at Fratton Yard. This train is made up of empty TTA tanks and timber traffic from Chichester, and is seen passing Paulsgrove. Cosham station is located around the curve in the distance. (PN)

Another of my favourite locations is the footbridge at the eastern end of Cosham station. Some interesting survivors of its past still survive here; for example, note the concrete rail supports for the cattle dock, while on the other side of the line the loading gauge still stands. No. 33058 on the Cardiff to Portsmouth Harbour chugs past. (PN)

Approaching Port Creek Junction from the Havant direction we have a good view of No. 33058 on an engineers' train made up of a long rake of Dace wagons, with a couple of Grampus types at the rear to spoil the symmetry. It was always nice to see something unexpected! (PN)

Racecourse Lane Bridge, back in the days before bridges had to have high fencing to deter vandals. Having passed Portchester and on its way to Pompey while working a train from Plymouth, a nice clear view is afforded of this Network 50, whose number eludes me. Traffic hurries along the M27, oblivious to the delights below. (PN)

Approaching Portcreek Junction from the Havant direction, one of Gateshead Depot's locos, No. 47415, is seen on an inter-regional train bound for the Harbour station in Portsmouth. This view was caught from the road bridge that provided access into the railway triangle in Cosham. (PN)

Over at the west side of Cosham, on the straight from Portchester station, a nice surprise is caught in the form of No. 33119, which is working a lengthy engineers' train, possibly to Three Bridges. The platelayers' hut looks rather unfinished. (PN)

After a long wait on the triangle at Farlington, at last No. 56034 *Castell Ogwr/Ogmore Castle* slowly passes on the Ardingly to Westbury ARC stone empties, which means I can rush back to work for the afternoon! (PN)

Heading for Havant, Sprinter No. 155307 runs up to Farlington Junction. These units coming into the area spelled the end of Crompton Class 33s on the Cardiff trains. The Class 155s were later split to make 153 single cars. (PN)

A nice view of No. 33011 on the Eastleigh to Portsmouth and Southsea (low level) mail train as it passes under Cornaway Lane Bridge. Portchester Crematorium is beyond the trees on the right; not a place you would like to visit, really. (PN)

The exchange sidings for MOD armament trains. Out from the depot comes army locomotive No. 222 with three VEA and three sheeted open wagons. These trains ran MWF only, so a variety could be observed as long as the MOD Police weren't in a bad mood. I was moved on only once though, with them saying that I was trying to photograph what was inside the wagons. I should have left my X-ray camera at home, I suppose. (PN)

Bedenham Sidings. Risking being charged with espionage, I had sneaked through the adjacent woods to capture the MOD train, which was waiting for the outgoing freight to arrive at the transfer sidings visible on the extreme right. Note that the tail lamp has been swapped, so the loco is ready to go on the rear of the train when it gets here. On this occasion, the Class 33/1 has delivered open wagons. (PN)

Powering away from Bedenham Sidings with its MOD freight, we have a nice look at Stewarts Lane's ED No. 73121 *Croydon 1883–1983*. This view shows a Blue Bus now, as the line was turned into a bus rapid transit (BRT) road, so there are no more MOD trains, unfortunately. (PN)

Wallington Viaduct plays host to No. 207010 as it runs towards Fareham. Some years previously, a light plane attempting to make a forced landing in the fields crashed into the other side of the viaduct and ended up a tangled heap. The viaduct was virtually undamaged. (PN)

The Coastway Crusader special at Fareham, with a replacement Class 33 for the failed 25 on nice-looking InterCity stock. Above the train, the dead-straight Gosport Branch line disappears into the distance, until it reaches the stop blocks at Bedenham. The failed 25 was dumped at Eastleigh Depot for a long time. (PN)

Fareham was still sunny when No. 33112 *Templecombe* rolled out of Funtley Tunnel with the parcels for Portsmouth, which once loaded would continue to Waterloo later in the evening. This is another of my favourite pictures. (PN)

A sunny Fareham welcomes No. 50041 *Bulwark* off the Netley line with a Plymouth to Brighton service. The loco looks a lot better than it did back in 23 November 1983, when it entered Paddington station on its side due to vandalism. (PN)

In what was the Gosport loop at Fareham, the short-lived Fratton to Didcot coal empties slowly pass on its way via Botley to Eastleigh and north to Didcot with its train of HEAs. On summer evenings it was possible to photograph what was a rare sight in the 1980s – namely, a Class 37 in Hampshire. (PN)

No. 55015 *Tulyar*, passing through Botley with the Wessex Deltic railtour on 17 October 1981. The railtour originated at Finsbury Park and visited Bournemouth, Eastleigh and Portsmouth. (JD)

USA tank No. 30064 is trundling through Eastleigh station on the Up fast line with a short freight in the early 1960s. The Southern Railway sign says 'Enginemen and others of the Locomotive Department are forbidden to walk along the railway between the station and the Loco Yard'. The sign, overhead gantry, signal box and the track on the right leading to the original Platform 1 are now part of history, having been removed many years ago. (Colin Rawlings)

British Railways Standard Class 4 2-6-0 No. 76062 is passing through Eastleigh in the early 1960s with a lengthy mixed freight, which is probably heading for Southampton Eastern Docks. This loco was one of a batch (No. 76053–69) that were fitted with the larger BR1B tenders for use in the Southern Region, where there were no water troughs. One of the new Class 33 diesels can be seen on the Up through main line. (Colin Rawlings)

In the summer of 1985, Class 45 Peaks provided regular power for the Severn Tunnel to Eastleigh Speedlink and return working. On 16 August 1985, No. 45041, minus its *Royal Tank Regiment* nameplates, is heading 6V83 (the 16.10 return working from Eastleigh Yard) to the station, where it will run round before taking the Chandlers Ford route to South Wales. In the background is 6E30, the 17.19 Speedlink departure to Dringhouses Yard. (JD)

Eastleigh Works forms the backdrop as No. 45034 leaves with the Eastleigh Yard to Severn Tunnel Junction Speedlink service. A pair of Cromptons rest alongside a Class 47 on the left, while lines of withdrawn electric units and rakes of bitumen tanks fill the sidings. This is my only record of Peaks at Eastleigh, as another two rolls of shots of them were stolen from the van carrying them to the developers – much to my chagrin! (PN)

On Saturday 7 September 1985, 4REP unit No. 3011 is leading two 4TC trailer units as it approaches Eastleigh. The train is 1B08, the 06.54 Bournemouth to Waterloo, and it bears the headcode 92, which was the semi-fast service. (JD)

Push-pull No. 33107 is approaching Eastleigh with the QE2 boat train from Southampton Eastern Docks to Waterloo on 4 June 1987. Headcode 95 indicates the Eastern Docks, while boat trains to the Western Docks were headcode 96. The stock is a dedicated rake of eight Mk 2 first-class coaches, with a blue GUV and two Mk 1 brake composites. (JD)

Eastleigh's famous Platform 3 witnesses LPG empty tanks leaving with Class 47 power for Furzebrook Sidings, working via Worgret Junction and the Swanage Branch. The Swanage Railway hopes to take over the now disused fan of sidings for its maintenance base in the near future. LPG was shipped from Furzebrook at the BP Wytch Farm oil field in Dorset to the BP LPG terminal at Hallen Marsh, Avonmouth. The LPG trains from Furzebrook to Avonmouth ran from 20 November 1990 until 22 July 2005. (PN)

Until the early 1990s, Class 37s were not seen in this area very often. This changed with the advent of rail freight sectorisation. In the early 1990s the Distribution Sector began using pairs of the class on some of the Southampton Freightliner workings. No. 37068 *Grainflow* and No. 37101, both in distribution livery, are seen passing through Eastleigh with 4L66, the 07.55 Southampton Maritime to Ripple Lane on 5 November 1992. (JD)

The Railfreight Metals Sector also started to regularly send Class 37s on the steel trains to Hamworthy from South Wales. On 7 June 1990, No. 37293 is seen passing through Eastleigh with 6O45, the 02.50 from Cardiff. The loco is in Metals Sector livery and has yet to receive its high-intensity headlight. Behind the loco is a good variety of steel wagons. (JD)

A busy scene at Eastleigh on 30 June 2012. From left to right the trains are: No. 444024 (in Platform 1 with the 10.50 Poole to Waterloo stopping train); No. 444003 (which is overtaking No. 444024 on the Up fast with the 10.20 Weymouth to Waterloo); No. 444027 (on the Down fast with the 11.05 Waterloo to Weymouth); No. 66118 (in Platform 2 and heading for the depot); No. 158886 (in Platform 2 with the 12.07 Romsey to Salisbury); and No. 377475 (in Platform 3, forming a Brighton to Southampton service). (JD)

A surprise move on 22 July 2009, when DRS No. 20306 was used to collect restaurant car No. 80042 from the docks to Eastleigh Works. Class 20s have always been unusual in this area and this is the only one I have seen working singly. It is seen here approaching the station with 5Z20, the 16.30 train from the docks. It will run up to the East Yard, where it will run round before coming down to the works. (JD)

No. 20132 *Barrow Hill Depot* and No. 20118 *Saltburn-by-the-Sea* are seen approaching Eastleigh with 5Z15, from Burton Wetmore Sidings, ready for the following day's railtour from London to Swanage. 7 September 2016. (JD)

No. 66714 *Cromer Lifeboat* approaching Eastleigh with 4Y19, the Mountfield to Southampton Western Docks gypsum. This service usually runs seven days a week. 7 September 2016. (JD)

In early morning winter sunshine, No. 47354 is at St Denys with the Whatley Quarry to Totton ARC stone. The roadworks are the making of the new Thomas Lewis Way, and the footbridge where I had previously taken many photographs is not long for this world in this shot from 27 November 1987. (JD)

The Glasgow to Poole overnight train was a short-lived service introduced in 1990. No. 47813 is passing through St Denys on 17 April 1991 with 1O03, the 21.20 from Glasgow. The consist comprises a BG, two Mk 3 sleeping cars and a Mk 2 open coach. (JD)

At St Denys, No. 33042 is about to pass with a long train of army vehicles, possibly on their way to Marchwood Military Port, which is accessed via the branch line to Fawley. This line is now disused beyond Marchwood, seeing that oil trains no longer serve the refinery. (PN)

Bevois Park was once an incredibly busy yard, with Transits from the Ford factory being loaded onto carflats here and other freight being received. The adjacent cement terminal also sent trainloads of cement presflos out regularly. Here, No. 33035, on the 09.46 Southampton Up Yard to Halling, Kent, winds out of the yard with the usual fifteen Rugby Cement PCAs. (PN)

No. 66130 is approaching Horseshoe Bridge at St Denys with 4V42, the 17.36 Southampton Eastern Docks to Morris Cowley empty car wagons. The return working is normally loaded with Minis for export. (JD)

In the days before Internet access, I had no idea that the Hunslet-Barclay weed-killing train would be running round here until it passed before my camera lens. No. 20901 *Nancy* takes the train back towards St Denys station, perhaps to take the Netley line. I hope it didn't go down the Gosport Branch that day. That would have been cruel. (PN)

No. 34052 *Lord Dowding* (renamed and numbered from No. 34046) is seen with 1Z48, the 18.11 Southampton Central to Clapham Junction via Selhurst. This train was put on as the Crystal Palace Football Club special for their final match of the season at Southampton. A smart rake of coaches follow, with Pullman car *Pegasus* as the third coach. The headboard reads 'Icons of Steam'. 15 May 2016. (JD)

Mount Pleasant Crossing at Southampton is always very busy. With its four running lines between St Denys and Northam Junction, road traffic can be held for up to fifteen minutes at peak times. The summer Saturday 16.10 Portsmouth Harbour to Cardiff Central was double-headed during the summer of 1981, and Nos 31145 and 31257 were providing the power on 29 August when seen passing under the semaphores. (JD)

A busy scene at Mount Pleasant on 17 January 2017. The main attraction is the test train being hauled by No. 37025, with No. 37099 on the rear. It is 1Q52, the 10.37 from Eastleigh Arlington to Eastleigh Arlington, which will travel via many of the local routes. About to overtake it is a Class 220 Voyager forming the 10.27 Manchester Piccadilly to Bournemouth. Going in the opposite direction is the 13.50 Salisbury to Romsey train, formed of No. 158884, while in the distance, No. 158953, with the 10.50 Great Malvern to Brighton, is waiting to cross to the Portsmouth line. (JD)

During 2015, a Railvac was based at Totton Yard; it is seen here at Mount Pleasant, heading to its home on 9 July. The working is 6Y56, the 10.35 from Butterley to Totton, and is hauled by No. 56104. The Railvac machine is used to remove ballast and soil from the track without it being lifted, and was also used for clearing drains. (JD)

GBRf No. 66721 *Harry Beck* is heading 4Y19, the 12.19 Mountfield Sidings to Western Docks Gypsum containers, when seen at Mount Pleasant on 8 August 2015. This loco was painted into this unique livery for the 150th anniversary of the London Underground. It has a Tube map on each side of the loco, one from 2013 and the other from 1933. (JD)

The first Class 70 diesel locos were built in 2009 and were put into service with Freightliner, who have a fleet of nineteen. The last one of the class, No. 70020, is seen at Mount Pleasant with 4M99, the 16.57 Southampton to Trafford Park Freightliner on 9 July 2015. Colas Rail have since acquired their own fleet of Class 70 locos. (JD)

Southampton Up Yard at Bevois Park had not been used for a few years when a stone-unloading terminal was introduced in 2014. The loaded stone trains came from the Peak District in Derbyshire about once a week, usually arriving around 09.00, with the empties heading north during the afternoon. On 17 August 2016, No. 66158 is seen arriving with 6O11, the 10.00 from Dowlow Briggs Sidings, which has taken almost twenty-four hours to reach Southampton, though it did spend a few hours at Wembley Yard during the small hours of the night. (JD)

No. 66177 is approaching Mount Pleasant crossing with 6Y32, the 08.24 Fawley to Holybourne empty crude oil tanks on 17 August 2016. (JD)

No. 66201 is waiting to leave Southampton Eastern Docks with the Solent Witness Railtour. From here it would head for the Western Docks, followed by trips down the Fawley Branch and the Hamworthy Branch. 28 December 2012. (JD)

On an unknown date in the early 1960s, 9F 2-10-0 No. 92153 has arrived in Southampton Eastern Docks to collect a freight train. This loco was not welcome in the docks due to the sharp curves, and apparently the local supervisor quickly sent it back to Eastleigh. (Colin Rawlings)

Class 67 No. 67029 was named *Royal Diamond* at Rugeley station on 12 October 2007 to celebrate the diamond wedding anniversary of the Queen and the Duke of Edinburgh. Seen here in its one-off silver livery, it is approaching the Canute Road level crossing in Southampton to gain access to the Eastern Docks with 1Z94, the 08.45 from London Victoria. 4 August 2009. (JD)

No. 47345 is heading 6B56, the 11.16 Fawley to Eastleigh, which is made up of empty 100-ton bogie crude oil tanks. It has just emerged from the tunnel under Southampton city centre and is about to take the sharp curve at Northam. The Class 47 is in the Railfreight grey livery, with the red stripe around the lower bodyside. 16 June 1988. (JD)

The double-track section through Southampton tunnel has reversible working as demonstrated by 4VEP unit No. 3075. The service is 2B27, the 10.42 Waterloo to Bournemouth stopping train, and it bears the headcode 93. The unit is in Network SouthEast livery. It was re-numbered from 7775 and is seen approaching the tunnel on 16 June 1988. (JD)

High-speed trains were a welcome sight in the area when they were used on some of the inter-regional services between the South Coast and the North. Power car No. 43065 *City of Edinburgh* is at the head of an InterCity-liveried set as it rolls into Southampton Central with the Virgin Trains 14.20 Bournemouth to Manchester Piccadilly, which was listed in the timetable as The Pines Express. 26 May 1998. (Steve Mosedale)

No. 66067 is approaching Southampton Central with a train of imported Renaults, forming the 6B44 from the Western Docks to Eastleigh Yard. At Eastleigh it will be remarshalled into the 6V38 wagonload service, which would run to Didcot and eventually to Mossend in Scotland. Tanks from Fawley and MOD wagons from Marchwood also used this service to travel north. 11 July 2013. (JD)

Thundering on the six-track section west of Southampton Central station, Hampshire DEMU No. 205030 makes a fine sight as it heads towards Millbrook in Network SouthEast livery. The headcode 44 shows this is a Southampton to Salisbury local service. The rail network was rather empty after the withdrawal of these units, but they call it progress! (PN)

Nos 33057 and 33107 have charge of 7V84, the 06.15 Three Bridges to Meldon Quarry empty ballast wagons. This was the main source of ballast for the Southern Region of British Rail. This train reached Eastleigh at 09.15 from the Fareham route and was staged in the yard, where the locos run round before departing at 12.35. It is seen here after passing through Southampton Central station. 11 April 1988. (JD)

No. 47582 *County of Norfolk* is in the original Network SouthEast livery. It has just departed from Southampton Central with the 07.45 Newcastle to Poole, where it will arrive at 16.15. 11 April 1988. (JD)

Exeter to Waterloo services were sometimes diverted through Southampton due to engineering work, but usually only on weekends. On Monday 11 April 1988, I was surprised to catch the diverted 11.05 Exeter to Waterloo at Southampton behind No. 50008 *Thunderer*. The early Mk 2 stock consists of a good mix of blue-grey and Network SouthEast liveries. (JD)

Looking along the multi-track section between Southampton Central and Millbrook, I had the good fortune of witnessing the Eastleigh breakdown train passing on its way back to base in the capable charge of No. 73111. (PN)

With good views in both directions, the footbridge at Millbrook station has always been a popular vantage point for photographers. Freightliner's No. 66591 is very near the end of its journey with 4O54, the 06.15 from Leeds to Southampton Maritime Terminal. The well-loaded wagons are a mixture of different types of container carriers. 3 May 2013. (JD)

Every few weeks a track-testing train visits the Southampton area. On 30 June 2016, this was 1Q23, the 13.39 Salisbury to Salisbury, which ran into the Southampton Up goods loop before reversing. On this occasion it was top and tailed by Nos 68020 and 68004. This was one of the first visits to this area by the Direct Rail Services Class 68 locos. (JD)

In its one-off Tata Steel silver livery, No. 60099 has charge of 6V38, the 11.00 Marchwood to Didcot wagonload service, containing just one loaded container wagon. Meanwhile, No. 70019 is engaged in assembling wagons in the Millbrook Freightliner depot. 14 March 2013. (JD)

In early Railfreight grey livery, with the large double arrows logo, is No. 47350 *British Petroleum*. It is working its way over the crossovers at Millbrook from the Southampton Maritime Freightliner terminal to the Up main line with the 13.05 departure to Coatbridge, near Glasgow. 22 March 1988. (JD)

After the 4REPs were taken out of service to provide power bogies for the new Wessex Electrics, double-headed Class 73s filled in on Weymouth to Waterloo services. These were much more photogenic, I'd say. I hope you agree. The locos are Nos 73109 and 73114, and they are busy powering a Bournemouth to Waterloo semi-fast headcode 92 service. (PN)

No. 33027 *Earl Mountbatten of Burma* is passing the Millbrook Recreation Ground with the 10.10 Cardiff Central to Portsmouth Harbour on 22 March 1988. This is a typical formation for these hourly services, which were usually made up of five Mk 1 coaches. These trains have been replaced by Sprinter units since 1991, and today are usually made up of three coaches, making it difficult to get a seat on some services. (JD)

The last regular vacuum-braked revenue freight in our area was the Llanwern to Hamworthy steel service. On this occasion, the train is mostly made up of SFV four-wheel steel coil wagons with canopy covers. It is hauled by No. 47280 *Pedigree* and is passing the Maritime Freightliner terminal on the right and the BOC Depot on the left. 3 July 1986. (JD)

A surprising sight of two of the EWS-liveried Class 60 locomotives, No. 60045 *The Pernament Way Institution* and No. 60049, are seen passing the Southampton Maritime Freightliner while working 6O41, the Westbury to Eastleigh Engineers service on 5 September 2013. At this time there were only three Class 60s still working in this livery, the other one being No. 60065. (JD)

6Z30, the 17.26 Westbury to Eastleigh service, is approaching Redbridge on 16 May 2014. This was one of the first local services to be powered by Colas Railfreight locos. On this occasion the locos are Nos 70807, 70805, 70801, 70806 and 66849, with JNA and MLA wagons. The extra locos were probably on a positioning move. The train was ninety-five minutes late and the sun had all but gone, so the photograph was taken at ISO 1600. (JD)

No. 60103 *Flying Scotsman* is captured on its first visit to Southampton since its recent overhaul. It is approaching Redbridge with 1Z82, which was a Salisbury to Salisbury trip via Southampton. Although the weather was unfortunately wet, there were large crowds out to watch it pass. 21 May 2016. (JD)

In 1990, No. 60011 *Cadir Idris* was the first Class 60 to arrive at Eastleigh Depot for local driver training. It is seen double-heading with Dutch-liveried No. 33118 at Redbridge with the lunchtime Fawley to Eastleigh oil train. 21 September 1990. (JD)

Narrow-bodied No. 33203 is crossing the River Test at Redbridge with 6O32, the 20.15 Longport to Fawley empty LPG tanks. These tanks were used to transport LPG to the potteries for use in firing the kilns. Eventually this fuel was replaced with natural gas, which caused the demise of these trains. 12 December 1986. (JD)

Royal Train loco No. 67006 *Royal Sovereign* has just left Redbridge with 7X19, the 04.40 Didcot to Marchwood MOD. It has a load of eleven Warwell wagons loaded with Warrior tracked troop carriers. This train arrived at Redbridge from the Romsey line and the loco ran round the wagons before proceeding across the River Test. 6 February 2013. (JD)

In 1986 there were two paths a week for stone trains to Totton, which were on Tuesday and Thursday. On 12 June 1986, Railfreight grey-liveried No. 56039 is at the unloading facility at Eling with ARC PGA wagons. This is only half of the train, as the wagons were split into two groups in Totton Yard, and two return trips were made down the short branch for unloading. The service is 6O53, the 09.10 from Westbury, and the return working is 6V31, which departed at 14.35. (JD)

Bombardier Voyager units capable of 125 mph replaced the Class 47-hauled cross-country services between Bournemouth and Manchester Piccadilly in the early 2000s. A Class 221 Voyager unit is passing Totton Yard on 26 February 2010 with 1O08, which left Manchester for Bournemouth at 07.27. (JD)

A busy scene in Totton Yard on 20 September 2014, 31601 and 31452 have arrived to pick up the Railvac which is booked to go to Chard later in the evening. 56103 is shunting the Railvac into position without its usual escort of open wagons. 56301 is stabled on the right hand siding. (JD)

No. 47099 is approaching one of the many level crossings on the Fawley Branch with 6B51, the 10.37 Eastleigh to Marchwood MOD Speedlink working on 20 June 1986. Behind the loco is a good load of Warflat and Warwell wagons loaded with various military vehicles and equipment. Bringing up the rear are a few air-braked vans. (JD)

On 4 July 2013, No. 60074 is seen passing the semaphores and level crossing at Marchwood with 6B93, the 09.38 Eastleigh to Fawley tanks. No. 60074, named *Teenage Spirit* in support of the Teenage Cancer Trust, is in a special light blue livery. (JD)

Colas-liveried No. 37116 with 1Q66, the 07.47 Eastleigh to Woking via Fawley test train, is seen approaching the station at Marchwood from the Fawley direction. Green-liveried No. 37057 is on the rear. 1 November 2017. (JD)

No. 33056 *The Burma Star* is approaching Marchwood with 6B72, the 13.15 Fawley to Eastleigh tanks with a mix of bitumen and diesel products. At the time this was a regular daily service, with the tanks travelling on to various locations from Eastleigh in Speedlink services. 26 June 1986. (JD)

In green livery, No. 45106 is spotted at Hythe with 1Z37, the Wessex Adventurer Railtour, which was run by Pathfinder Railtours and ran from Manchester Piccadilly to Fawley. Nos 33114 and 33102 were attached to the rear for the run down the branch and they pulled the tour back to Southampton. It then proceeded down the main line to Weymouth. 5 November 1988. (JD)

No. 47231 *The Silcock Express* in Railfreight Distribution livery is at Hythe with the 13.35 Fawley to Eastleigh tanks on 28 April 1988. Photography is not possible in this area anymore due to the growth of the lineside vegetation. (JD)

Network Rail test trains are booked to visit the Fawley Branch from time to time, but they do not always seem to reach the end of the branch; some I have been told are due to no signalman being available for the level crossing, and others due to the train running late, with the Fawley Branch thus being missed. It was good news then when Network Rail-liveried No. 31233 arrived at Frost Lane level crossing in Hythe with 1Q07, the 10.03 Selhurst to Bournemouth via Fawley. On the rear was No. 73107, which would lead the return working. Monday 19 April 2010. (JD)

Every summer for the last few years, steam-hauled day trips have run from London to Weymouth or Swanage. On 23 August 2017, No. 60009 *Union of South Africa* is seen speeding through the New Forest at Deerleap with 1Z67, the 08.14 Victoria to Weymouth Dorset Coast Express. (JD)

No. 33105 is seen heading south through the New Forest towards Beaulieu Road on 15 June 1982. The wagons are BP 45-ton oil tanks and are carrying fuel oil for the vessels at Weymouth Quay. The working is 6W63, the 07.06 Hamble to Weymouth Quay. (JD)

37409 *Lord Hinton* and Inspection Saloon 975025 *Caroline* at Beaulieu Road on 22 June 2012. It is 2Z02, the 08:50 Kensington Olympia to Weymouth and return on its southbound trip.

In Railfreight Distribution Sector livery, No. 47049 is approaching Beaulieu Road with 6W51, the 08.03 Eastleigh to Wareham Speedlink, consisting of two empty Tiger PBA china clay hoppers. The wagons would be loaded with ball clay at Furzebrook for transportation to the potteries via the Speedlink network. 13 August 1990. (JD)

No. 66522 is seen at Beaulieu Road with the 6O49 Neasden to Wool empty sand hoppers. No. 66522 is in a one-off Freightliner Shanks livery. 3 June 2013. (JD)

A Class 450 unit is seen heading through the forest at Beaulieu Road on 13 May 2015. These South West trains, in their bright blue livery, are normally used on the stopping services to and from Poole. (JD)

When I was a schoolboy at Brockenhurst in the early 1960s, it was a highlight to see a non-Southern loco. The 09.20 from Birkenhead to Bournemouth West would pass after school and was usually headed by Western Region Hall Class 4-6-0, or occasionally a Grange. It is seen here at Beaulieu Road, being hauled by No. 6976 *Graythwaite Hall*. (Colin Rawlings)

Colas locos are not seen very often on the main line through the New Forest, so it was a welcome sight to see No. 70804 with 6C15, the 08.09 Eastleigh to Worgret ballast, at Beaulieu Road on 25 August 2015. (JD)

The weed-killing train is approaching Beaulieu Road when seen on 16 June 1989. It is hauled by one of the narrow-bodied Class 33/2s – No. 33202, in Railfreight Construction livery. (JD)

General Motors No. 59203 has just passed Beaulieu Road station with 7O51, the 06.11 Westbury to Hamworthy loaded stone wagons on 4 May 2018. This was usually a once-a-week service and was the last regular freight working through the New Forest. Since this date, it has ceased to run. The loco was one of six originally built for National Power in 1995, and since been taken over by DB Cargo.

No. 73141 *Charlotte* and No. 73136 head 6G22, the 06.00 Dorchester to Eastleigh ballast, with Nos 73212 and 73213 on the rear. All four locos are in GBRf livery. 9 September 2014. (JD)

Bulleid Pacifics ruled the Bournemouth line from 1948 until electrification of the route in 1967. In this view, preserved Merchant Navy No. 35028 *Clan Line* has just passed Beaulieu Road with 1Z67, the 09.52 Waterloo to Bournemouth, complete with the Bournemouth Belle headboard and VSOE Pullman coaches. This train was run to celebrate fifty years since the end of everyday steam-hauled trains on this route. 5 July 2017. (JD)

Once the Bournemouth line was electrified, the express passenger services were handled by 4REP and 4TC units. Class 430 4REP unit No. 3012 is seen here heading a classic formation of a 4REP plus two 4TC units across Bishops Dyke in the New Forest with the 07.34 Weymouth to Waterloo service. The rear 4TC unit would have been pushed from Weymouth to Bournemouth, where it was added to the front two units. 5 July 1979. (JD)

The Class 442 Wessex Electric units, which were introduced in 1988, replaced the 4REP and 4TC units on the Bournemouth trains, and then to Weymouth with the extension of the electrification. Two of the five-car 442s are seen here heading south at Beaulieu Road with 1W29, the 16.32 Waterloo to Weymouth. They will split at Bournemouth, with the front unit going through to Weymouth. 16 June 1989. (JD)

Desiro unit No. 444032 is leading a ten-coach formation at Woodfidley in the New Forest. The service is the 09.35 Waterloo to Weymouth, which split at Bournemouth, with only the front five-car unit continuing to Weymouth. After privatisation, the Class 442 Wessex Electric units were replaced by these Class 444 Desiro units by South West Trains. 26 September 2009. (JD)

Stone trains have run to Hamworthy Quay from the Mendip quarries on and off since the 1990s, usually being hauled by Class 59 locos. On 1 April 2009, No. 59104 *Village of Great Elm* is at Woodfidley in the New Forest with 6O48. The 09.22 from Whatley Quarry. (JD)

No. 33013 is heading north at Woodfidley on a 1975 Sunday evening with the twice weekly Motorail service to Stirling in Scotland. The train is 1M63, the 20.35 from Brockenhurst, and is composed of four coaches, a brake second open, a corridor first, two sleeping cars and six carflats. It will call at Kensington Olympia, where it will be combined with a similar formation from Dover, making a lengthy train for the overnight run up the West Coast Main Line as the 1S15 to Stirling. (JD)

Class 458 Juniper units are not normally seen in this area. However, as they were being withdrawn from service for conversion, a farewell tour was run on 23 May 2015. Units Nos 458006 and 458014 were used on 1Z45, the 09.02 London Waterloo to Poole railtour, which is shown here as it approaches Platform 1 at Brockenhurst for a short leg-stretch stop for its passengers. (JD)

The Network Rail measurement train was formed with ex-Virgin high-speed train power cars in 2003. It tours the network, carrying out track inspections. On 17 June 2010, it is seen arriving at Brockenhurst as 1Q23, the 14.51 Basingstoke to Old Oak Common via Weymouth. The leading power car is No. 43014, while No. 43062 *John Armitt* is on the rear. (JD)

The weekend of 22 and 23 May 2010 saw the final runs of the two Class 421 3-CIG slam-door units on the Lymington Branch. Unit No. 1497 *Freshwater* is seen departing Platform 1 at Brockenhurst with yet another full train of enthusiasts. The headboard reads 'Slamdoors say Farewell to the Lymington Flyer'. *Freshwater* was one of the Isle of Wight car ferries used by British Railways between Lymington Pier and Yarmouth from 1959 until 1984. (JD)

South West Trains Class 450 units are used on the Lymington Branch at weekends instead of the Class 158 diesel units, which are used from Monday to Friday. On Saturday 16 August 2017, the 17.57 from Lymington Pier is seen arriving at Brockenhurst, headed by No. 450024. (JD)

No. 33019 is approaching Lymington Junction with 6W61, the 06.24 Eastleigh to Poole mixed freight, which is made up of vacuum-braked wagons. This train would soon be replaced by a Speedlink working made up of higher-capacity air-braked wagons. 9 May 1980. (JD)

2HAP units were the mainstay on the Lymington Branch in the early 1980s, with 4VEP units taking over at weekends. 2HAP unit No. 6024 is seen crossing Setley Plain with the 07.57 Lymington Pier to Eastleigh on 9 May 1980. (JD)

No. 158880, forming 1J21, the 11.12 Brockenhurst to Lymington Pier, is seen heading across the heathland at Setley on 3 September 2014. During the last few years, Class 158 two-car diesel multiple units have been used on the branch on weekdays, with four-car Class 450 electric units being utilised at weekends. (JD)

The Lymington Branch celebrated 150 years in use on 12 and 13 July 2008. No. 73109 *Battle of Britain 50th Anniversary* was attached to 3-CIG unit No. 1498 *Farringford* for the weekend and is seen at Setley with a service from the pier to Brockenhurst. (JD)

Lymington Town station, as viewed from the car park, showing a selection of 1970s cars. This is where I would go to purchase my Runabout ticket in the early 1960s, before then catching the push-pull train to Brockenhurst. (Ray Kingswell)

3-CIG unit No. 1497 *Freshwater* is crossing the iron bridge over the Lymington River with a service from Brockenhurst to Lymington Pier on 22 May 2010. This was the final weekend of the slam-door units on the branch and most of the trains were full to capacity. (JD)

Green-liveried 3-CIG unit No. 1498 *Farringford* is seen arriving at Lymington Pier during the slam-door weekend with a service from Brockenhurst. *Farringford* and was one of the British Railways car ferries that ran between Lymington Pier and Yarmouth on the Isle of Wight from 1948 until 1974. 22 May 2010. (JD)

The New Forest ponies are oblivious as No. 33104 passes with the empty VSOE Pullmans of the Beaulieu Belle, heading for Bournemouth for servicing. It has just departed from Brockenhurst, where the passengers were transferred to coaches for their afternoon visit to Beaulieu and the National Motor Museum. 27 August 1983. (JD)

BR Standard Class 4 2-6-0 No. 76025 is at Lymington Junction with a train from Bournemouth West to Brockenhurst via the Ringwood route. This loco was allocated to Eastleigh Depot and is probably running in place of an M7 tank. The coaches are Maunsell push-pull set No. 608. (Colin Rawlings)

A view of Holmsley station, showing the shelter on the Up platform. The bridge carries the A35 road, and the trackbed is now a road linking Brockenhurst to Burley. (Colin Rawlings)

An undated view of Holmsley station buildings, which are on the Down side of the tracks. This is now a very popular tea room, complete with some railwayana. (Colin Rawlings)

Class 3 2-6-2 standard tank No. 82029 with a two-coach Maunsell push-pull set stands at Ringwood station. As this is not a push-pull-fitted loco, it will have to run round its stock at Brockenhurst. (Colin Rawlings)

No. 47495 has just passed through Sway with a Sunday morning Up engineers' train. The train is made up of a variety of vacuum-braked four-wheel wagons, most likely carrying spoil or dirty ballast from the previous night's work on the line. 22 January 1978. (JD)

It is not very often we see a Deltic in this part of the country, so No. 55009 *Alycidon* was a welcome visitor when seen on 21 October 2017. The occasion was a day trip from Burton-on-Trent to Swanage, and this view shows the return working at Sway, which was 1Z55, the 15.08 from Swanage. Following the generator coach is a smart rake of Mk 2 coaches in BR blue and grey livery. The photograph was taken in fading light, with the camera set at ISO 2000. (JD)

Another local freight working that no longer runs is 6M42, the 11.13 Wool to Neasden loaded sand. This was a Freightliner working and on 14 May 2014 No. 66508 was providing the power when seen approaching Sway station. (JD)

Battle of Britain Pacific No. 34067 *Tangmere* was a regular performer on steam specials to and from the Dorset Coast from 2009 to 2015. It is seen here turning heads and shattering the peace and quiet of New Milton with 1Z67, the 08.44 Victoria to Weymouth Dorset Coast Express. 27 August 2014. (JD)

No. 47445 is seen approaching Hinton Admiral station with the summer Saturday 07.57 Weymouth to Bradford on 7 July 1979. (JD)

A pair of Class 73/1s, Nos 73107 and 73116, have plenty of power as they form 4W22, the 11.50 Poole to Waterloo parcels, consisting of five vans. The train is seen passing through Hinton Admiral station on Sunday 20 January 1980. (JD)

For the first time in five years, the stone trains from Whatley Quarry in Somerset started running to Hamworthy at the beginning of 2017. DBS-liveried No. 59204 is at Hinton Admiral with 6V52, the 12.05 Hamworthy to Westbury returning empty stone wagons on 19 April 2017. (JD)

No. 33043 is at Bournemouth, waiting to leave for London with the VSOE Pullman Bournemouth Belle on 12 July 1986. This train, named the 'Beaulieu Belle', had been running on selected summer Saturdays since 1983, terminating at Brockenhurst with a coach connection to Beaulieu. The earlier runs had produced smart and quite often named Class 33 locos, but standards had slipped by this time. (JD)

Another lucky shot; this time, No. 47381 is seen passing through Branksome station on 6W62, the 11.55 Furzebrook Wytch Farm to Fawley Refinery crude oil train, which will reverse at Southampton to gain the Fawley Branch at Totton. These trains ended when a pipeline was built. It is nice to see the clean Class 47 in Railfreight Petroleum livery on the front. (PN)

Unfortunately, with electrification reaching Weymouth, the Class 33/1s on Bournemouth to Weymouth push-pull trains were about to end, so an expedition to record them had to be carried out. This is Branksome, with what I believe is No. 33117 propelling past the fine signal box at the junction. (PN)

Hope springs eternal! My wife said 'Lets go to Poole and look at the shops', so with reluctance I agreed. Luckily I took the camera, and when we got to the crossing the gates came down. As luck would have it, No. 58036 came round from Poole station with the Furzebrook to Hallen Marsh LPG tanks. The driver is seen waving to the crowds, who on this occasion were not trying to cross with the gates down – which apparently happens a lot, despite the presence of a footbridge. (PN)

Desiro No. 444037 is seen at Holes Bay, Poole, with 1W16, the 11.03 Weymouth to Waterloo on 31 March 2016. (JD)

The Swanage Railway ran a Bulleid steam gala in the spring of 2017 with five Bulleid Pacifics working passenger and freight trains. There were two rebuilt locos: No. 34052 *Lord Dowding* (renumbered from No. 34046) and No. 34053 *Sir Keith Park*. The other three were originals: No. 34070 *Manston*, No. 34081 *92 Squadron* and No. 34092 *City of Wells*. Resident Battle of Britain *Manston* is making a steamy departure from Harmans Cross with the 13.40 Swanage to River Frome when seen here. The first coach is Car No. 14, and was one of the two ex-Devon Belle Pullman observation cars. 1 April 2017. (JD)

The 2018 Swanage Railway diesel gala included green-liveried No. 73133 and No. 73136 *Mhairi* in GBRf livery. The pair are seen here at Harmans Cross with the 12.15 Norden to Swanage on 13 May 2018. (JD)

In March 2014, the Swanage Railway held a London & South Western Railway weekend. On 15 March, two LSWR locos are seen meeting at Corfe Castle: M7 No. 30053 is waiting to leave with the 10.46 to Norden, while T9 No. 30120 is approaching with the 10.40 Norden to Swanage. (JD)

Hymek D7017 was a welcome visitor to the three-day-long Swanage Railway diesel gala held from 11 to 13 May 2018. On Sunday, and wearing its smart green livery, it is seen accelerating away from Corfe Castle towards Norden with the 16.45 from Swanage. Pullman observation car No. 14 is behind the loco. (JD)

A nice scene at Wool station as a headcode 91-carrying Class 33/1 arrives from Bournemouth. I don't think I would fancy using that stepladder like the chap on the top, as it looks like it has had some repairs. You would think one of the men stood there would steady it! (PN)

No. 33118 is at Wool with the Weymouth Quay to Waterloo Channel Island boat train on 5 August 1983. The Class 33 will only take the train to Bournemouth, with a Class 73 electro-diesel then taking over for a fast run to London, stopping only at Southampton Central. (JD)

As part of a visit to Weymouth and other areas of Dorset, the queen and Prince Phillip travelled down on the Royal Train, which is seen here approaching Bincombe Tunnel with the royal visitors on board. As would be expected, the locos top and tail the set, with No. 67006 *Royal Sovereign* leading and No. 67005 *Queens Messenger* on the rear. 11 June 2009. (Mark Jamieson)

An Arriva Trains Wales Class 150 is sandwiched between First Great Western Class 153 and 150 units at Bincombe with an Up train from Weymouth. 11 August 2009. (Mark Jamieson)

The old road to Weymouth provides a great view of No. 33117 rolling down the grade from Bincombe Tunnel with the two 4TC sets that form the Weymouth portion of the train from Waterloo. The third rail that will banish the Class 33s from Dorset can be seen in place. (PN)

With a sunlit Weymouth in the background, Railfreight grey-liveried No. 37691 is heading up past Wishing Well Halt towards Bincombe Tunnel with the 16.58 Weymouth to Cardiff on 30 August 1990. This is a summer-only service, on which freight-only locos were often used. (JD)

Nearing journey's end at Weymouth, and passing the site of the lamented Weymouth Steam Depot, we have a nice view of No. 33115 nearing the station environs. Note the EMU in the sidings; they will banish the Cromptons to history when the third rail is fully activated. A sad day, in my opinion. I'll miss them. (PN)

One of Cardiff Canton's DMMUs, set No. C854, rolls into one of Weymouth's surviving platforms and passes piles of old concrete and a derelict signal box – not a nice welcome for travellers coming to enjoy the seaside delights. I never got to see any activity on the harbour branch, but thankfully John did. (PN)

Hertfordshire Railtours' InterCity Merrymaker–Weymouth Awayday stands at Weymouth. The locos are No. 31128 *Charybdis* and No. 31452 *Minotaur*, both in matching Fragonset livery. InterCity-liveried No. 31545 *The Heart of Wessex* is on the rear. The train was running as 1Z31, the 18.18 Weymouth to Minehead on 26 August 2007. (Mark Jamieson)

A Class 33/1 is waiting time at Weymouth station with a departure composed of a 4TC set, which it will push as far as Bournemouth to be added to the rear of a Waterloo-bound train. (Ray Kingswell)

An unidentified Class 33/1 is crawling along the Weymouth streets to the quayside with the Channel Island boat train. It is led by two flagmen to clear the route and warn pedestrians and traffic of the oncoming train. (Ray Kingswell)

1W15, the 09.40 Waterloo to Weymouth Quay Channel Islands boat train, is crawling along the streets of Weymouth on the branch to the quay. The Class 33/1 loco, No. 33117, has a bell fitted to the buffer beam and is passing under the Town Bridge. This is a section of line prone to flooding on very high tides. 6 August 1983 (JD)

No. 33117 is seen alongside the platform of Weymouth Quay station on 6 August 1983. It has run round the stock of the incoming boat train and will return to Waterloo at 14.30, with the train reporting code 1W34. The Sealink Channel Island ferry MV *Earl Granville* is beside the quay. (JD)